FROM JAWS TO CLAWS

WOLF

Written by Eliza Nodes

Gareth Stevens
PUBLISHING

Published in 2026 by
Gareth Stevens Publishing
2544 Clinton St.
Buffalo, NY 14224

Written by: Eliza Nodes
Edited by: Rebecca Phillips-Bartlett
Designed by: Amelia Harris

Cataloging-in-Publication Data

Names: Nodes, Eliza.
Title: Wolf / Eliza Nodes.
Description: Buffalo, NY : Gareth Stevens Publishing, 2026. | Series: From jaws to claws | Includes glossary and index.
Identifiers: ISBN 9781482475999 (pbk.) | ISBN 9781482476002 (library bound) | ISBN 9781482476019 (ebook)
Subjects: LCSH: Gray wolf--Juvenile literature. | Gray wolf--Life cycles--Juvenile literature. | Wolves--Juvenile literature. | Wolves--Life cycles--Juvenile literature.
Classification: LCC QL737.C22 N634 2026 | DDC 599.773--dc23

Printed in China

CPSIA compliance information: Batch #QW26GS: For further information contact Greenhaven Publishing LLC at 1-844-317-7404.

Image Credits
Images courtesy of Shutterstock.com, unless otherwise stated.
Cover – Vlada Cech, EvaLes, Kwaczek. Recurring – Lars Poyansky, Anutikgon, Binimin, Elena Pimukova, Impixmart. 2–3 – Alexandr Ryabinin, bieszczady_wildlife. 4–5 – Michael Roeder, Bjarne Henning Kvaale, Don Mammoser, Geoffrey Kuchera. 6–7 – Jearu, shymar27. 8–9 – Ray Hugo Tang, Willy Mobilo, slowmotiongli. 10–11 – Alfmaler, Nature's Charm, FCG. 12–13 – Michal Ninger, Kjetil Kolbjornsrud. 14–15 – Hanna Kipel, Volodymyr Burdiak. 16–17 – Vishnevskiy Vasily, Geoffrey Kuchera. 18–19 – Ondrej Prosicky, Holly S Cannon. 20–21 – Jennifer Herrera, DebraCarr. 22–23 – Bildagentur Zoonar GmbH, A.von Dueren.

CONTENTS

WORDS THAT LOOK LIKE THIS CAN BE FOUND IN THE GLOSSARY ON PAGE 24.

THE WOLF

Wolves are known for their haunting howls. They live in groups called packs. Most packs have between four and ten wolves. A wolf pack is usually a family with the parents as the leaders.

Wolves are found in lots of different habitats. They can live in forests, deserts, and mountains. Wolves can live in hot, dry places and in cold, snowy areas.

JAWS AND TEETH

Wolves are predators, which means they hunt prey to eat. Wolves have very powerful jaws. This helps them to crush the bones of their prey, such as moose and deer.

Adult wolves have 42 teeth. The four longest, sharpest teeth are called canines. They can grow up to 2.3 inches (6 cm) long. Wolves use their canines to grip their prey.

A PAWESOME FACT

A WOLF'S CANINES ARE OFTEN KNOWN AS FANGS.

EYES AND EARS

Wolves have excellent eyesight in the day and at night. This helps them hunt for prey during cold winters. Young wolves have blue eyes. As they grow up, their eyes turn a yellow or golden color.

Wolves can hear noises from 5.5 miles (9 km) away in the forest and 10 miles (16 km) in the open. Their hearing is not just for hunting. If they are separated from their pack, they howl to find one another.

NOSE

A wolf's sense of smell is around a hundred times stronger than a human's. They can smell prey from almost 2 miles (3 km) away. However, snow can make it harder for wolves to smell their prey.

Wolf packs live in areas called their territory. One pack's territory can be thousands of miles wide. They use their smell to mark their territory. This stops other wolves from coming into it.

A PAWESOME FACT

WOLVES MARK THEIR TERRITORY BY PEEING, RUBBING, OR SCRATCHING ON TREES AND ROCKS.

BODY

An adult wolf can grow up to 6.5 feet (2 m) long. Their slim body helps them with their running and swimming. Wolves use their bodies to communicate their feelings to each other.

If wolves are feeling happy, they hold their heads and tails up high. If they are feeling scared, wolves bring their bodies closer to the ground. They then put their tails between their legs.

FUR

Wolves have two layers of fur. The layer on the outside protects the wolf from water and snow. The inside layer is thick and soft to keep the wolf warm.

A PAWESOME FACT

IN SUMMER, WOLVES SHED THE INSIDE LAYER TO KEEP COOL.

Gray wolves are the most common type of wolf. Their fur coats can range from white to black, but most are gray or light brown.

TAIL

Wolves have long, fluffy tails. This helps them balance when they are walking. In cold habitats, wolves may use their tails to keep their faces warm when sleeping.

At the base of their tails, wolves have a scent gland. They use it to mark their territory. Wolves often sniff these glands when they meet each other.

THIS WOLF IS SNIFFING THE OTHER WOLF'S SCENT GLAND.

LEGS

Wolves can travel around 50 miles (80 km) a day looking for food. Their long legs help them take big steps to cover a lot of ground quickly.

Wolves can walk long distances at 5 miles (8 km) an hour. They can run short distances at about 37 miles (60 km) an hour. They usually run at this speed to catch prey.

PAWS AND CLAWS

Wolves have big paws. Big paws stop wolves from sinking into the snow. Each toe pad is surrounded by hairs. This keeps their feet warm.

A PAWESOME FACT

WOLF CLAWS ARE MADE OF KERATIN, JUST LIKE HUMAN FINGERNAILS.

A wolf's claws grow throughout its life, just like fingernails. Their claws are very thick and strong. Wolves mainly use their claws for digging and for grip when running.

LIFE CYCLE

Female wolves are pregnant for around two months. They usually give birth to four to six babies. They are called pups. Pups that are born at the same time are called a litter.

A PAWESOME FACT

LIFE CYCLES ARE THE STAGES LIVING THINGS GO THROUGH DURING THEIR LIVES.

Wolf pups are born with dark fur. After six months, their winter coats start to grow. When they are 11 months old, they start hunting with their pack.

A PAWESOME FACT

WOLVES IN THE WILD CAN LIVE BETWEEN FIVE AND TEN YEARS.

GLOSSARY

COMMUNICATE to pass information between two or more things

GLAND a body part that makes chemicals

HABITATS the natural homes of plants or animals

PREGNANT when a female animal has one or more young or babies growing inside her

PREY animals that are hunted by other animals for food

SHED when an animal loses its fur

TERRITORY an area claimed and defended by an animal group

INDEX